Lost at Sea

Written by
Rob Waring and **Maurice Jamall**

Before You Read

to dive			marina	
to paddle			rope	
to swim			shelter	
anchor			stone	
engine			storm	
fire			wave	
island			wind	
			wet	

In the story

 David

 John

 Faye

 Tyler

 Daniela

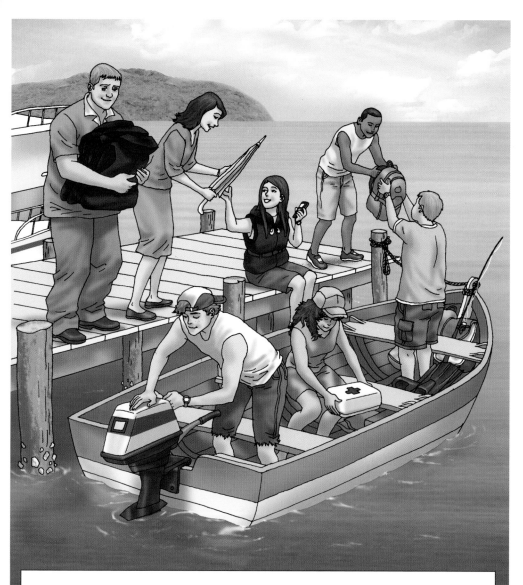

"Faye, please take this. It may rain later," says Faye's mother.
"Yes, Mom," she says. Faye's mother gives her an umbrella.
Faye, and her friend, Daniela are in Bayview Marina. They
are going on their boat with their friends David, Tyler, and
John. They are very excited because they all love to go to
many islands in their boat. Today, they are going swimming.

"Do you have everything?" asks David's father.

David replies, "Yes, we have everything, Dad. Thanks. We have all the swimming things."

"And I have my new phone," says Faye. She shows it to her mother. "I can call you any time."

Faye's mother smiles, "That's great. Take care, and don't do anything dangerous, okay? Have a good time. Bye!"

"Okay, Mom," says Faye. "We'll be back at 4 o'clock."

They leave Bayview Marina and take their boat out. They often go swimming. John, Faye, and David like to go diving.
"Let's swim here," says David. "This is a great place for diving. It looks fun."
"Okay," says Tyler. "John, put the anchor in, please," he asks.
"Okay," John replies. He puts the anchor into the water.

"Come on, John. Let's get in the water," says Faye.
"It looks great!"
Faye and John dive down into the water. The boys
swim around the boat and play in the water. They
are good swimmers. Tyler tries to catch fish, and
Daniela watches John and Faye. David goes into
the water, too. They are all having a great time.

Later, Faye looks at her phone. She says, "I just had a call from my mother. She says a storm is coming. My mother wants us to go back."

"Oh really?" says John. "But I want to stay longer."

Tyler says, "But John, there's a storm coming. It's dangerous in this small boat in a storm. Let's go. David, please pull up the anchor and let's get back to the marina."

"Sure," David replies.

David tries to pull up the anchor. But it will not move.
"Tyler! The anchor!" says David. "It won't come up.
It won't move!"
Tyler says, "What? Oh no! I'll help you! John, can you
help, too?"
John, Tyler and David all pull on the anchor, but the
anchor does not move. They pull many times, but the
anchor still does not move.

"What do we do, now?" asks David. "Think of something."
"Cut the rope," says Daniela. "We must get back. And the storm's coming."
Tyler cuts the anchor rope. Faye is looking at the storm coming towards them.
"It's getting darker. And the storm's coming fast," Faye says.
"It's getting nearer, and nearer."
The wind is very strong. Then it starts to rain.

The rain and the wind are getting stronger, and the rain is getting heavier.

"I don't like this," says Daniela. "Let's go back. I want to go home."

David says, "Me, too!"

"It's okay," says John. "We'll be okay." But John is worried.

They are all worried. The rain is very heavy and they cannot see.

"Which way is the marina?" asks Faye.

"I don't know now. I can't see," answers Tyler.

Tyler starts the boat engine. He takes the boat back to the marina, but he cannot see very well. The rain is very heavy. It does not stop. Water is coming into the boat now. Everybody is getting more worried. The waves are pushing the small boat.

"I can't see," says Tyler. "The rain's too heavy. We'll never get back to the marina."

"Maybe it's this way!" says David. "I can see something. Let's go this way."

The small boat hits something very big in the water. Faye, John and Daniela fly out of the boat. They go into the water. David falls into the bags, and the bags fall into the water.

"Oh no! The bags!" says David. "Get the bags! Quick!" Everybody gets wet, but they are all okay.

They get back in the boat but they are very wet and cold now. "Is everybody okay?" asks Faye.
Daniela says, "Yes, I'm okay. But my leg isn't," she says.
Tyler says, "I'm okay. John looks okay, too."
"I'm okay. But look!" says David. "The bags are all wet."
"Oh no!" says Faye. "My bag!"

Faye looks into her bag. "Oh no! My phone's wet," says Faye. "It doesn't work! I can't call home."

Tyler says, "And the engine isn't working now. It's broken. It won't start."

"Oh no!" says Daniela. "What can we do?"

"There's only one thing to do," says Tyler. "We must paddle the boat to the marina. And let's paddle fast!"

They paddle for a long time in the wind and rain.
"Tyler, where are we?" asks Daniela. "I'm scared."
"Daniela, I don't know, I have no idea," replies Tyler.
"We may be lost."
It is starting to get dark and it is still raining. They are cold
and wet. They are very tired. They cannot call for help.

The waves are pushing the small boat. They are in big trouble. John and David take the water out of the boat.
"Maybe we're going the wrong way," says Daniela.
Suddenly, John says, "Look, there's an island. Can you see it? Let's go to it."
They all paddle to the island. It is hard work. The wind is too strong, and the waves are very high. They paddle harder and harder.

After a long time, they get to the island. They get out of the boat. It is nearly dark, but it is not raining now.

"We were lucky to find the island. I'm happy we're off that boat!" says Daniela.

David asks, "Yeah, me too! But where are we?"

"I don't know," says John. "This may be Shark Island. Or it may be Bear Island. We were in the boat for a long time."

"What do we do now?" asks Daniela. "We can't call for help. Nobody knows we're here."

Faye has a plan. She tells her plan to the others. "It'll be dark soon. We stay here tonight," she says. "We need a shelter, some wood, a fire, some stones and some water. I'll make the shelter. Who wants to help?"

"I'll help to make the shelter, too," says Tyler.

David says, "Can I help you?"

John says, "I'll get some wood and I'll make the fire, and I'll get some stones."

Daniela says, "I'll get some water."

They all start to work. David and Tyler make the shelter with Faye. They work very hard.

"It's not good, but it'll be okay," says Tyler.

The shelter is not big but everybody can get in it.

"It's nearly dark. Be quick, everybody," says Faye.

Faye helps John make the fire.

Soon, the shelter is ready and there is a big fire. Daniela and David are getting some water.

"What are you doing, Daniela?" asks Tyler.

Daniela says, "We're getting some water so we can have it later."

"That's a good idea," Tyler says.

It's dark now and everybody is still cold. David says, "I'm still wet."

John says, "I can't sleep. I'm too cold."

"Come over here near the fire," says Faye.

"Let's sing some songs," says Daniela. "Does anybody know *Shining Star*?"

They all start singing and they feel better.

The next morning, they are cold and tired. They did not sleep well.

Daniela hears something. "Listen," she says. "What's that?"

"Look. It's the police helicopter!" shouts Tyler. They are all very happy to see the helicopter.

"We're here. We're here. Help! Help!" shouts David.

"Don't shout," says Faye. "They can't hear you!"

"Oh no! The helicopter is going away. Come back!" says Daniela. "What are we going to do?" she asks.

Faye says, "Everybody, get some stones! Help me put some stones here."

"Why, Faye?" asks John.

"There's no time. Get some stones, please. Big stones, not little ones. And be quick, everybody," she says.

John says, "But Faye . . . , why?"

"Now! Just do it!" she says. "Get some stones!" They run to get some stones. They write *SOS* with the stones.

Soon, the police helicopter comes back. Daniela shouts, "Help! Help!"
Faye's mother and David's father are in the police helicopter. They see everybody on the beach.
"They are coming for us," David says. "We're okay now!"
John says, "We're safe! We're safe!"
"What an adventure," says Tyler.
"But I don't want to do that again!" says Daniela. They all laugh.